LIFE IS GOOD

To Karen
Please enjoy the
Words i Write
they come from
my heart.

Love
Letha

LIFE IS GOOD

Letha R. Owens

Prospect Press
Sistersville
West Virginia

Copyright © 1999 by Letha R. Owens

All rights reserved. No part of this book may be reproduced or transmitted in any form or by any means, electronic, mechanical, photocopying, or otherwise, without the permission of the publisher and the author.

Published by Prospect Press
609 Main St
Sistersville, West Virginia 26175

Library of Congress Catalog Card Number:
    98-067739

ISBN: 1-892668-07-6

Manufactured in the United States of America

First Edition

10 9 8 7 6 5 4 3 2 1

Life Is Good

*Life is so good at this time
now I drink my glass of wine.
Cheers to me it's way overdue
now the laughter is shining through.
Happy at last what can I say
I'll live life my own way.
So many people I've yet to meet
life right now is a treat.*

Dedicated to

My loving sister who gave me a place to stay, when I thought all was lost. She gave me inspiration, the love I needed so desperately, when I had no one to turn to. The one who always listened to my words even when they didn't make sense.
Thank you Carole for being there.

Marla: the dearest friend for the past twenty-seven years and counting. Where would my life be without you, my dearest friend? Pages nine and nineteen I dedicate to you.

All my love
Letha R. Owens

Contents

The Journey 1
Dying Flower 2
Oh Mommy 3
Words I Write 4
Lasting Moments 5
Are You Out There 6
Hand Of An Angel 7
Many Thoughts 8
Best Friends 9
My Boys 10
My Cookie Girl 11
She 12
Angel Dear 13
Flickering Candle 14
Walk Away 15
Listen To The Trees 16
Smiles 17
Little Lady 18
When I Need You're Always There 19
The Road He Walks 20
A Job Well Done 21
The Key 22
Flowers 23
Happy In The End 24
Wings Of An Angel 25

Never To Explain 26
Field Of Flowers 27
Father Dear 28
Harley Man 29
We Miss You So Much 30
A Loving Child 31
Do I Dare 32
Oh Daddy 33
Dreams Of You 34
Old Man 35
Need A Smile 36
Blue Eyes 37
Grow Old With Me 38
Tears Of The Past 39
Dreams 40
Your Eyes 41
Green Frog 42
Heaven At Last 43
Footsteps In The Snow 44
I'm Always Near 45
Hard To Let Go 46
Last Time 47
Crowded Room 48
The Thrill Of It All 49
Treasured Memories 50

LIFE IS GOOD

The Journey

Come take my hand and walk with me.
Life has a journey for us to see.
Together we'll talk and share our dreams.
A lot of plans or so it seems.

Don't let go hang on to me
I'll be here if you need
A helping hand to guide you through
All the days that seem so blue.

🥀 *Dying Flower*

*Lay your head upon my breast
let me feel that warm caress.
The feeling rushing throughout me
if you look close you will see.*

*The calmness you put on my face
you've taken away any trace
Of the sadness so deep inside
you set me free no longer to hide.
The dying flower comes alive!*

    Thank You Kevin

Oh Mommy

*Oh mommy can't you see
how mean this man is to me.
I cry for help but you never listen
and yes there is something missing.
The love we shared once before
then he walked in and you closed the door.
You take his word what can I say
it's been clear since he came to stay.
Now I must tell you how I feel
time can only help me heal
My broken heart so deep inside.
These are the things I will no longer hide.
Mommy I love so much please help me.*

*Emily my heart cries for you
I'm always here*

All my love Nana

Words I Write

*These special words I write to you
come from a heart that was sad and blue.
Until the day you walked in,
you gave me life once again.
How can I thank this special man
who's always there with helping hands.*

Lasting Moments

Every time I see that smiling face
It reminds me of our special place.
You only come once in awhile.
But oh how nice to see that smile.

We talk and tell each other many things
sometimes we talk about our dreams.

If only we could reach our goals.
Will we know what they hold?
Time passes by way too fast
remember our words, and make them last.

🌹 Are You Out There

I hear a whisper soft and low
I see a face, I do not know.
You walk in the shadow of all my dreams
who's this man I have not seen.
Are you real I cannot say
I see my dreams slipping away.
If you come to me, in the dead of night.
I know the power will be right.
We all have dreams we don't understand.
Please make my dream part of
Your plan.

Hand of An Angel

An open path a hand held out.
The blazing fire left no doubt.
The hand of an angel reached out to you.
To save your life and guide you through.
Come take my hand the water is waiting.
Pain so great life seemed to be fading.
A long hard battle you must endure.
The water of the soul is so pure.

Thank you for sharing your story with me.
It touched so deep inside, I had to write this for you.

🌹 *Many Thoughts*

*The heavens, the moon, the stars above,
there's nothing on earth that compares to
    the love
I have for you and always will
writing about you is such a thrill.
To tell everyone about this man
I hold so dearly in my hand.
He needs much love and tender care
always looking for someone to share
His thoughts, his dreams, and so much
    more
She waits for that knock on the door.*

Best Friends

I see you now and remember you as a child
Oh so young, and oh so wild.
Now you're grown with kids of your own
Making plans in your happy home.

The man you love is right beside you
With ups and downs he'll guide you through.
The love you give is never ending
I thank God above for sending

Someone like you, into my life.
To my best friend till the day I die.

My Boys

I see the stories in your eyes
when you talk of your boys
they come alive.
The smile you give, it shows so much
always a father, with tender touch.
Two loving boys with so much to give
a loving father that only lives
For his boys throughout life
what he gave up he never thought twice.
Now this man is old and gray
his sons are with him to this day.
If only in his thoughts and mind
these are the memories, that are so divine.

My Cookie Girl

*You came to me when you were two
and wanted a new name what to do.*

*We thought for awhile, and I said with a smile
I'll call you cookie what do you think
you said you loved it, and gave me a wink.*

*I'll call you cookie till my days end
you read this and remember when.
We talked and laughed and had so much fun
I'm your Nana and you're number one.*

All My Love Nana

She

*Hair so golden, eyes so green,
This little girl has so many dreams.*

*She found a love after so many years.
Can she ever stop the tears.
Sad and alone much of her life
Someone's mother someone's wife.*

*Now she's old and on her own.
She carries this burden all alone.
The time has come for happiness at last.
She tries not to think of the past.*

Angel Dear

The light that shines down on me
the angel has come for all to see.
To life my spirits and take them to so high.
As my thoughts float to the sky.
Then we wonder where they go
the angel says take them slow.
If you need I'll always be here
raise your hand, I'm always near.
Just call my name angel dear.

Flickering Candle

*The flickering candle in my mind
tells me things I cannot find.
Where to look and what to see
is this light only for me.*

*It seems to guide me through the worst of
    times.
It lets me know, that things are fine.
Flickering candle never die
you give me peace, to keep me alive.*

*I'm a good person and some day
you'll see, all the good inside of me.*

Walk Away

I see the foot steps walk away
I know in my heart there's nothing to say.
Never to see your face again,
never to see that silly grin.

The things you said are so deep in my
   mind.
Tugging at heart strings I could not find.
I now must go on another road,
only to carry that heavy load.

Of letting you go, was so hard to do
now I must go start anew.
Life with someone who wants to share
life with the one, who will be there.

🥀 *Listen to The Trees*

*I listen to the spirit, who speaks to me
it seems to whisper from the trees.
I'm not through with you my dear
I'm here to help through all the tears.
Hold on to life and don't let go
always remember, to take it slow.
Time passes by way too fast
grab the moments and make them last.
We are sent here, to do many things
never forget, your hopes and dreams.
I thank this spirit every day, it sends
kindness in every way.
If you are as lucky as I
the spirit will take you to the sky.*

Smiles

The sweat pouring down, over your face
the way you move, that hidden trace
Of the love you make through the night
you send me spinning, out of sight.

To open my door and you standing there
what you're thinking, and wanting to share.
You captured my love and the rest of me
now open your heart and let me see.

If I can get in, I'll stay for awhile and
always promise to make you smile.

❦ *Little Lady*

*Little Lady pushes her cart from corner to
corner looking for a place to lay her head.
She has no home or a bed.
Her eyes tell so much if you look deep
  within
The wrinkles show the pain and that's not
  a sin.
She lost her family, home and more
the day she walked through the door.
Never to return or look back,
what she owns is in her sack.
The cart she pushes is all she has left
she'll push the cart until her death.*

🌹 When I Need You're Always There

*When I look back through the years
at all the laughter and the tears.
My dearest friend always there
with words to comfort and time to share.*

*There are no words that can describe
my dearest friend so deep inside.
Never to judge and always there
to give advice and always be fair.*

*Please share my friendship until the end
I ask only this from my dearest friend.*

🌹 *The Road He Walks*

The common thread that seems to bond
he searches for love all around.
He yet not knows what waits for him
the love he has and wants to send.

His caring touch reaches out for some one
to hold, at last his story can be told.

He goes through life with no one to
share, no one to love, no one to care.
His life half over and almost gone
This road he walks all alone.

A Job Well Done

The dancing wind that blows through me
the day so clear for all to see.
Who's to say what's right or wrong
do we know when to play that song.
Of what life has waiting for us
we know the word must be trust.
How can we trust when we do not know
and why must we always put on a show.
Is it hard to really care and can we ever
    learn to share.
If you find that certain one, tell yourself
    a job well done.

8/2/96
2:00 a.m.

The Key

The lock we keep upon our chest
keeps us safe from all the rest.
No hurt, no pain, we have not felt.
Through it all we tell ourselves.
Life has dealt us a wonderful thing
it's called sharing, now let it begin.
What you do with it, is all up to you
the key to life, is always be true

To yourself and you will find
that life is sharing, till the end of time.

Thank You Kevin
You Gave Me The Key!

Flowers

The garden path I slowly walk.
The flowers at my side seem to talk.
They tell me to get on with the rest of my life.
Around the bend there is a surprise.

What it is, I yet not know, but the flowers
tell me to walk very slow.
Take some time to pick a few,
smell the scent and wipe off the dew.

Also the tears from your eyes,
forget old loves and the lies.

🌹 *Happy In The End*

*You're the best friend to come in my life
I no longer sacrifice.
You bring out thoughts I keep in my mind
locked away for all time.
So alive you make me feel, I keep asking
are you real.
You are so funny and talk so much,
just to feel that loving touch.
The words you speak set me on fire,
in my face you see desire.
Please tell me some day
we'll be more than friends
I'll make you happy in the end.*

Wings Of An Angel

The wings from an angel spread so wide
I can't say or try to hide
The helping hands she gives to me
it touches my soul and sets me free.

To guide me through the good and bad
she lets me touch what I've never had.
I think of my angel every day,
I thank her so much in that special way
For all the happiness I have today.

Never To Explain

*I look in the mirror, what do I see
a much wiser woman, staring back at me.*

*Now it's time for a brand new life
No looking back or thinking twice.*

*Peace at last I carry alone
upon my shoulders I must be strong.
I now walk free of guilt and pain
answering no questions never to explain.*

Field Of Flowers

*A field of flowers we run through
as life passes by too soon.
We pick a flower every day
we pick a love only to say
I choose you to be the one
to share my life till life is done.
The dreams we have can come true
only if we want them to.
So give me a flower only to say
I love you so much and want you to stay.
As life passed by and we grow old
always to love, always to hold.*

Father Dear

*Oh Father dear you're gone at last
to the great beyond you have passed.*

*There's so much sadness in my heart
to let you go, now we must part.
The memories we have will always be clear.
I say to you Father dear
Go at last only in peace, to the heavens
above you will sleep.*

Forever Lasting In My Thoughts

Harley Man

*The night so dark and the sky so blue
down the street the Harley flew.
The rider got off and to my surprise
the man I've waited all my life.
He took my hand and led me through
a night of passion I never knew.
To this day he's at my side
never to leave or say good-bye.
I thank my stars and heavens above
for sending you for me to love.
If the day should come when you choose
    to leave
Just remember I was here to please.
I'll pick up the pieces and move on
my Harley man was here and now he's
    gone.*

🌹 *We Miss You So Much*

*So many years have come and gone
since you passed to the great beyond.
You took your last breath on this day
peace at last I only pray.*

*Not a day goes by I think of you
And all the pain you went through.
To be so strong and love so much
all was blessed by your touch.*

*The loving mom that everyone knew
is now our angel shining through.*

A Loving Child

This tiny child has captured my heart
my first grandchild is ready to start
A life of love and so much to learn
a loving nana at every turn.
I'll always be here just call my name
always to listen and never to blame.
So many years have passed us by
my loving Emily still by my side.
All the little things you made for me
are on my wall for all to see.
So many memories we have yet to share
your loving nana will always be there.
With open arms and words to guide
the love we have and can't describe
my loving granddaughter still at my side.

Do I Dare

The sun shining down on your face
do I see a tiny trace
Of hidden love that no one can see
is this love only for me?
Take me in your arms and say what you will
touch my lips and feel the thrill
Of a lost love only to share, but do I love,
do I dare.

🥀 *Oh Daddy*

*These words you speak to me
they hurt so bad can't you see.
You tell me things I don't understand.
All I needed was helping hands.
How could you not love me any more.
You left my life and closed the door.
Now you tell me you're not my Dad
My life destroyed and heart so sad.
I loved you so much through years.
Do I deserve all these tears?*

Dreams Of You

I dream of you so much of the time
What we share is so deep in my mind.
I can't let go but you want me to.
Sadness so deep, eyes so blue.
Tell me now there may come a day
in your life I'll always stay.
Please take my hand we'll walk away
to love each other in that special way.

Old Man

*I see an old man tattered and torn
the clothes he has on, are so worn.*

*I stopped and talked to this old man
I could see there was something by his hands.*

*His face so soft yet old and frayed
I knew this man's life had been saved.*

*He was sent to me on this day
the old man and I walked away.*

🌹 Need A Smile

*Little things mean a lot
to the ones we love and have forgot.
To say I love you and give a smile.
For your love I'd walk
a mile, and back again
just to say, I love you so
much in every way.*

🥀 Blue Eyes

*If you read on you'll understand
why I love to keep this man.
The moment I saw those blue eyes
I had to meet this wonderful guy.
I put out my hand and said to him
eyes that blue should be a sin.
As I gracefully told my name
all the words came out the same.
Slurred and mumbled, could he understand
that's when he put out his hand.
We took a ride on that night
laughed and talked until day light.
Things I must say, have never been
the same since that day.*

🌹 *Grow Old With Me*

*Grow old with me and I promise you
The time we share will always be true.*

*Some day we'll go through the garden again
Talking and laughing remembering when.*

*The first time we met I must say,
you captured my heart in every way.*

Tears of the Past

My flames of friendship will always burn.
Maybe some day it will be my turn
To open my heart and let you in
for you to say let it begin.

The thrill of loving someone like you,
The tears of joy come shining through.
Just to know you're at my side, never
to leave or say good-bye.
This is the love I want to last
with no more tears of the past!

Dreams

Man of my dreams please come to me
I'm here waiting under the willow tree.
Golden hair blowing in the breeze
icy green eyes that always please.
If you look deeply they tell so much
move in close for that loving touch.
Under her spell you'll never win
she'll fight for you until the end.
The girl of your dreams is standing here
with love for you so warm and pure.

Your Eyes

Eyes so blue they captured my heart.
Open your arms I'm ready to start.

The love affair that is so hot
say the words ready or not.
If it's not right we'll find
out some day.
Tell me how nice along the way.

Sometimes my pen takes over me
it writes the words I want you to read.

Green Frog

While driving down the road
One day
I saw something laying not far away.
I slammed on my brakes and came
To a halt
Jumped out of my car without a thought.
Much to my surprise, a little green
frog before my eyes.
The frog said to me it's a nice day
don't you think?
Then he gave me a little frog wink.
I knew right then this was meant to be
The little green frog and little ole me.
We'll go through life, happy as can be.

Heaven At Last

*I softly walk on this cloud
down below I see a crowd.
People looking up in the sky
I now have wings, now I fly.
Please grant this wish I pray to you
don't clip my wings, I'm not through.
The power so strong I feel in my heart
my new wings, my new start.
A whole new life on this night
if you could see this beautiful sight.
Flying so high all alone, I know
by now, I must be gone
To a better place in the sky
you know by now we all must die.*

Footsteps In The Snow

*Stop and smell the flowers
on this fine day.
You never know, what may
come your way.
Look at life through blue
eyes, and don't let her love
pass you by.
For if you do let her go
you'll only see footsteps
in the snow.*

I'm Always Near

*Will I ever find a man who can
love and understand
The needs I have and want to share
love so strong for one who cares.*

*I want some one who's sweet and kind
but always knows his own mind.
Some one to laugh and hold me tight
always there to say good night.*

*The words you speak I hold so dear
reach out and touch, I'm always near.*

Hard To Let Go

I see the footsteps walk away
I know in my heart there's
nothing to say.

Never to see your face again
never to see that silly grin.
The things you said are clear
in my mind.
Tugging at heart strings I could
not find.

I must go on another road
only to carry this heavy load.
Of letting you go was hard to do
the time has come to start anew.

Last Time

The tide has come in one last time
at last my life will be fine.
So many years with nothing to say
how could life turn out this way.

Now I look back through the years
through all the beatings and all the tears.
I stayed with you as long as I could
I wanted to leave but never would.

Then one day I opened my eyes
to all the deceit and all the lies.
Life alone would give me a chance
one last time, to do my dance.

❧ *Crowded Room*

*I see you across the crowded room
looking for someone to be with soon.*

*Take a look before your eyes
here I stand it's no surprise.*

*Take me now, I'm all yours
We'll leave together and close
all doors.*

🌹 The Thrill Of It All

To write about you is such a thrill
I see your face and get a chill.
You bring out the best inside of me
oh so happy for all to see.

Maybe some day you'll open your eyes
I'll still be here by your side.

Just call my name I'll be right there
a life together and so much to share.

🥀 Treasured Memories

*You hold a special place in my heart
now we know we must part.
To say good-by to the one we love
also thanking the stars above.
For sending you if only for awhile
to open my heart and make me smile.
To fill my life with so much pleasure
these are the memories I'll always
treasure.*